TEEN LIFE™

FREQUENTLY ASKED QUESTIONS ABOUT

Drinking and Driving

Holly Cefrey

ROSEN
PUBLISHING®

New York

Published in 2009 by The Rosen Publishing Group, Inc.
29 East 21st Street, New York, NY 10010

Library of Congress Cataloging-in-Publication Data

Cefrey, Holly.
Frequently asked questions about drinking and driving / Holly
Cefrey.—1st ed.
     p. cm.—(FAQ: teen life)
Includes bibliographical references and index.
ISBN-13: 978-1-4042-1809-3 (library binding)
1. Teenagers—Alcohol use. 2. Drunk driving—United States.
3. Drinking and traffic accidents—United States. I. Title.
HV5135.C45 2009
363.12'514—dc22

                                                            2007051056

Manufactured in the United States of America

Contents

WHAT IS ALCOHOL ABUSE?

Alcohol has been part of human society for thousands of years. Alcohol is used during times of joy, such as a wedding celebration. It is also used during times of sadness, for example, when mourning a death. It is used as part of social rituals that bring people together—family dinnertime at home, a meal at a restaurant with friends, a business lunch to seal a deal. It is used to stimulate social interaction, such as at clubs and bars where people go to dance and meet other people. It is used to relax after a long day at work and to wash away many of the stresses of daily living.

According to the United States Department of Health and Human Services (HHS), almost half of all Americans over twelve years of age (109 million people) reported in 2001 that they were alcohol drinkers. Alcohol use is so common that it is easy to forget that alcohol is a drug—a very dangerous drug.

In the United States, alcohol is the most commonly used drug. It is also the most commonly abused. According to HHS, about one in four children younger than eighteen years old is exposed to alcohol abuse or alcohol dependence in the family.

When a person abuses a substance, it means that he or she uses it improperly. There are right ways and wrong ways to use alcohol. Binge drinking—or drinking more than four or five drinks during a single occasion—is one of the wrong ways.

Underage Drinking

Drinking illegally, before you turn the legal age to drink, is another wrong way to use alcohol. Presently, every state prohibits the sale of alcohol to persons under the age of twenty-one. Nevertheless, according to HHS, people under the age of twenty-one find it easy to obtain alcohol. Often, underage drinkers consume alcohol not for social rituals but for a single purpose: to get drunk. About 10.4 million teens between the ages of twelve and twenty use alcohol, even though it's illegal for them to do so. Maybe you drink alcohol, too. If you drink regularly, you will need more and more alcohol to feel drunk on a single occasion. This means you are at risk of becoming a binge drinker.

Because it's illegal, underage drinking is usually done in secret. This can lead to isolation; drug dependency; trouble at home, school, and work; or life-altering conditions resulting from accidents or alcohol poisoning. According to the National Center on Addiction and Substance Abuse at Columbia

Though the legal drinking age is twenty-one, many young people manage to buy alcohol anyway and, as a result, engage in drinking and driving.

University, alcohol is involved as a factor in the three leading causes of teenage death: accidents, homicide, and suicide.

Think about that. The top three things that cause teens to die are related to alcohol in some way. So it's not as simple as just getting drunk—illegally or otherwise. And it's clearly not that easy to control. Each year, alcohol abuse contributes heavily to traffic fatalities and to domestic violence. Of course, it also causes alcoholism, a disease that affects millions of Americans. Alcohol abuse is often a factor in criminal behavior and in unplanned or unwanted sexual activity. Some of this sexual activity accounts for the dramatic spread of sexually transmitted diseases (STDs) among teens.

Alcohol Explained

Many of us think about alcohol as either of two substances: the kind you drink or the kind you use to sterilize things. Actually, there are more than a hundred different kinds of alcohol, and almost all of them are toxic (poisonous) chemicals that definitely do not make you drunk. Methanol, which is found in products like hairspray, aftershave, and nail-polish remover, can cause blindness and brain damage after a few sips. Paint thinner is another product that contains dangerous alcohols. These alcohols are not anything you would want to drink—they are extremely poisonous.

The kind of alcohol that people drink is called ethyl alcohol, or ethanol. Beer, wine, whiskey, rum, vodka, tequila, and gin are just a few kinds of beverages that contain ethyl alcohol. Large amounts of ethyl alcohol, or ethanol, can act as a poison. So while it may not be as toxic as the other kinds of alcohol, ethanol is still a potentially life-threatening, poisonous substance.

Ethyl alcohol is made by a process known as fermentation. In fermentation, grain, fruit, honey, or other foods containing sugar are mixed with yeast. Yeast, which are living organisms, consume the sugar and produce carbon dioxide and ethyl alcohol as waste products. In wine, the sugar comes from grapes. In rum, the sugar comes from sugarcane. In vodka, the sugar comes from potatoes. Other alcoholic beverages might use the sugar

There are many brands of alcohol. The three main types, though, are beer, wine, and liquor, such as whiskey and vodka.

from wheat and other grains or from fruits such as apricots, cherries, and plums.

Why Drink Poison?

Because of its nature, alcohol will always be a controversial subject. Yes, it's a poison. The real problem is dealing with the mixed messages that we get. Is alcohol good or bad?

Your parents or guardian may warn you about alcohol, and yet you may see it being consumed frequently. A parent or guardian may even seem more relaxed or happy when drinking. What's important to remember is that there are responsible ways and irresponsible ways to consume alcohol.

If you are over the age of twenty-one and have a glass of wine with dinner or at a party, you are not exhibiting signs of alcohol abuse. You may want a drink to feel relaxed, or you may believe that the taste of the wine enhances your meal. If you stop drinking before getting drunk, you are drinking the right way.

However, if you feel that the alcohol is necessary to enjoy yourself, then you're getting into a tricky area. There is a huge difference between want and need. A need is essential to survival;

There is a big difference between drinking to excess and drinking in moderation. People who drink legally and responsibly may have no more than a glass of wine with dinner.

a want is a desire. We can take or leave our wants, but we seek out our needs. When a person feels he or she needs a drink, it's a sign that the alcohol is more than a casual desire.

chapter two

WHY IS DRINKING AND DRIVING DEADLY?

Every day, people are maimed, scarred, burned, and paralyzed in accidents caused by drivers who are impaired (unable to function normally). Those victims who survive their accidents are the lucky ones. According to the National Highway Traffic Safety Administration (NHTSA), in 2004, more than 14,400 Americans lost their lives in accidents caused by people who were driving drunk or impaired.

The important issue about drinking and driving is that it is a matter of choice and is therefore preventable. It is a choice to drink, and it is another choice to drive. When the two are combined, the results can be deadly, especially for teen drivers, who are not as experienced as older drivers. According to the NHTSA, an average of three teens are killed each day when they make the choice to drive after drinking. This means that hundreds of young lives are cut short every

Drinking and driving doesn't just put you at risk. It endangers the lives of those who are in the car with you as well as other drivers sharing the road.

year by drunk driving. It is the number-one killer of young Americans between the ages of fifteen and twenty, according to the NHTSA.

Clearly, drinking and driving can be dangerous. If you hurt someone else while trying to prove you can drink and drive, you'll regret it the rest of your life. Drinking and driving can bring about other negative changes in your life. You could get a ticket, lose your license, or total your car. In addition, you could lose the trust of your parents or guardians as well as your friends, and it's not easy to reestablish that trust.

Teen Driving Can Be Dangerous

Even driving sober is dangerous. Studies show that teens face more risks than any other age group. According to the Insurance Institute for Highway Safety (IIHS), sixteen- to nineteen-year-old drivers are four times more likely to have a crash than older drivers. The National Safety Council claims that teen drivers are involved in 14.8 percent of fatal crashes, even though they make up only 6.6 percent of the total number of licensed drivers. This means that teens are involved in more than twice the number of fatal accidents as you'd expect.

The U.S. Centers for Disease Control and Prevention (CDC) states that in 2004, two out of every five teen deaths were caused by a car crash. As a teen driver, you are especially at risk for accidents because you do not have years of driving experience, and you may react improperly to sudden problems on the road. You're also more likely, according to the CDC, to run red lights and do illegal turns and actions, which increases the risk of a crash.

Passengers, too, die because of inexperienced teen drivers. According to the IIHS, in 2004, teenage drivers caused 62 percent of teenage passenger deaths. The risk for accidents increases when teen drivers have young passengers in the car. Some teen drivers think it's cool to be reckless and try to impress their friends by speeding, tailgating, or passing other cars in oncoming traffic. Loud music and talk, cell phones, electronic games, and text messaging are other distractions that can lead to accidents.

Much like talking on your cell phone, drinking and driving impairs your ability to pay attention to traffic and coordinate the road.

Try not to be lulled into a false sense of security by telling yourself that you're a good driver and that you can handle any type of traffic incident that you may encounter. Even if you are a great driver, you have to watch out for the bad drivers out there who may hit you. New drivers should always be especially careful driving and should use good judgment when deciding if it's safe to drive. According to *Dateline NBC*, the first five hundred miles a person drives are the most dangerous. Teens are ten times more likely than adults to crash during this initiation period on the road.

Alcohol: Is It Your Problem?

Monitoring the Future (MTF) is a major survey funded by the National Institute on Drug Abuse (NIDA). Each year, the MTF survey provides data on substance use among American youth. According to the latest survey, by the end of high school, at least 80 percent of the student population had tried alcohol. That means four out of every five students. When you think of five of your friends, how many of them have already tried alcohol? Are you one of them? If alcohol has become a part of your life, it's good to learn more about it and the increased risks you will encounter. The good news is that the choice is really up to you.

Alcohol consumption has powerful effects on young bodies and minds. The National Center on Addiction and Substance Abuse found that people who drink before the age of fifteen are four times more likely to become dependent on alcohol than those who begin at the age of twenty-one. If you are dependent on alcohol, you feel that you need it every day in order to survive. Alcohol dependency is actually a disease, called alcoholism. Teens are not immune from alcoholism. According to Focus Adolescent Services, there are an estimated three million teen alcoholics in the United States.

Adults and teens who drink are more likely to engage in risky behavior, such as drunk driving. In a 2003 CDC study, 30 percent of teens said that they had recently ridden in a car with a driver who was alcohol-impaired. One in eight teens said that they themselves had recently driven after drinking alcohol. Deciding to take these risks can bring about horrific consequences.

Alcohol abuse is the first step on the path to drinking and driving. Intoxication affects your ability to think clearly and make smart choices, such as staying off the road.

Learning the real deal about drunk driving and its dangers is the first step in making sure that it won't become your problem. You may even be able to help friends who you suspect may have drinking problems. If one of your friends is drinking and driving, you need to get help for him or her. Your friend isn't a bad person, but your friend needs to know that drinking and driving puts people at great risk of danger or death.

WHY DOES ALCOHOL MAKE YOU LOSE CONTROL?

Alcohol—even a small amount— dulls your senses and reflexes, impairs your vision, distracts you, and may make you hyper, drowsy, or aggressive. The same goes for any kind of drug, even prescription and over-the-counter medication. In short, drugs and alcohol make you a serious menace to yourself and others. You may think a short trip in your car while impaired isn't risky, but your passengers, other drivers, cyclists, and pedestrians may be forever affected by this "short" trip.

As a rule, you shouldn't drink at all if there is any chance you will be getting into a car and driving. Moreover, you shouldn't get into a car with anyone you suspect has been drinking—whether a teen or an adult—unless they are a passenger. In fact, you shouldn't let anyone who you suspect has been drinking

If you can't control your own body and mind as a result of alcohol, you certainly can't handle a moving vehicle.

get into a car and attempt to drive it, even if you're not riding with that person.

Why Is Alcohol Harmful to Your Body?

The things that you put into your body will affect the way it functions. For example, eating nutritious foods will make your body healthier than it would be if you ate lots of junk food. Alcohol and other drugs are toxic (poisonous), so putting them into your body can make you sick.

Alcohol is a poison, but it also has effects that many people find pleasurable. Alcohol is a psychoactive drug, meaning it alters the way you think and feel. Alcoholic beverages—used in small amounts—often produce an increased sense of well-being and sociability. People in this condition are said to "have a buzz" rather than "being drunk," which is a more advanced state of alcohol use.

If a drinker is seeking that buzz and drinks on a regular basis, more alcohol will be needed each time to feel the same effect. This is an example of tolerance, or when our bodies get so used to a substance that more is required for it to have any effect. Once the drink count has grown to four or five in a single occasion, the drinker is considered an alcohol abuser, and the casual act of drinking has become an addictive disease. Once a person is addicted, he or she will feel depressed or sick without the drug. Recovering will be a long and difficult process.

Alcohol affects many different bodily functions. This is because alcohol is absorbed into the bloodstream. From there, it

Alcohol reacts with your brain in a way that makes you feel happy and uninhibited. Though you may feel good, this overconfidence can be deadly when you have car keys in your hand.

affects the brain and spinal cord, which control nearly all bodily functions. While drinking alcohol, you'll experience slurred speech, problems seeing straight, and mood swings. As you become drunk, your coordination, judgment, memory, and reflexes will all be impaired. You may even become unconscious or pass out.

Blood Alcohol Concentration

As you drink, your body tries to get rid of the alcohol. It is not unusual for a drinker to take in alcohol faster than the body can get rid of it. At that time, alcohol that the body can't get rid of begins to build up in the bloodstream. The amount of excess alcohol in the blood is known as blood alcohol concentration or blood alcohol content (BAC).

Even your first drink can produce an increase in BAC. Your BAC can be measured by taking a sample of your blood. BAC also can be measured in your breath. BAC is expressed in percentages, such as .01 percent or .08 percent. A reading of .01 percent tells police or doctors that the drinker has about 10 milligrams of alcohol per 100 milliliters of blood. A reading of .08 percent means you have about 80 milligrams of alcohol per 100 milliliters of blood.

According to Mothers Against Drunk Driving (MADD), a BAC as low as .02 percent affects a person's ability to drive a car. This would be equal to about one or one and a half drinks. If you're pulled over by the police while drinking and driving, the police can measure your BAC very easily using a Breathalyzer test. Any percentage of BAC will indicate to police that you may have been drinking, even if it isn't obvious that you're drunk or impaired.

Losing Control of Your Car

In order to drive a car, you need coordination, balance, concentration, vision, sound reasoning and judgment, and sharp reflexes. To drive well, you need to use all of these skills effectively.

Reaction time is how quickly you respond to something. Slamming on your brakes, pulling to the side of the road to avoid hitting a car, or honking your horn all take a split second to do.

Alcohol slows down your ability to perceive and understand what's going on around you. Drugs take away that split-second ability to see, decide, and react, making an accident difficult to avoid.

According to researchers at Brown University, a blood alcohol concentration (BAC) of .05 to .06 will produce a decrease in reaction time. Your fine-muscle coordination, such as blinking and simple movements also begins to slow. At .07 to .09, you'll be showing obvious impairment in the ability to react to things, as well as an inability to actually know that you're impaired. According to researchers at the General Atomics Sciences Education Foundation, a BAC of just .04 percent will produce effects on your simple reaction time. At .08 percent, your slowed reaction time and impairment make you four times more likely to crash than if you are sober.

Peripheral vision is the ability to see things that are not right in front of you but at the sides of your field of vision. Houses, other cars, street signs, bike riders, and pedestrians pass on both sides when you are cruising down the road. You need to be able to see when another car pulls out of a driveway or intersection, or when the car next to you pulls up to change lanes.

A person with a BAC of .05 percent shows a loss of almost one-third of his or her peripheral vision on a field-of-vision test. This BAC is about one or two drinks in two hours for most people. The faster you drive, the more blurred your peripheral vision becomes, and the less able you are to see things off to the side.

Divided attention involves paying attention to several things at the same time. When you are driving, your brain must react to all of the things you see in front of you. Think about it: traffic

SOMETIMES IT TAKES A FAMILY OF FOUR
TO STOP A DRUNK DRIVER.

MADD

INSURANCE FOUNDATION AND GOLDEN VALLEY HEALTH CENTER.

Mothers Against Drunk Driving, or MADD, posts advertisements such as this one to convince people how devastating drunk driving can be.

lights, street signs, merging and exiting traffic, passing cars, steering, fiddling with the radio and turn signals, the glare of the sun or the lights of oncoming vehicles. There are dozens of things that require your attention, and alcohol makes it far more difficult to pay attention to several things at once.

Night vision is your ability to see when it is dark. Driving at night requires more caution and concentration than daytime driving. At night, we become half as able to see things. Alcohol reduces the oxygen in your bloodstream, which affects your vision. You drive with even less night vision than when you are sober.

Tracking skills are what allow you to guide your car along the curves of a road. Alcohol affects your brain's tracking skills, leading to an inability to follow curves and stay in your lane. This is why drunk drivers swerve between lanes and on and off the road.

Signs of a Drunk Driver and How to Handle It If You See One

If you're on the road and see the following things done by a driver, safely get to the nearest phone and call the police with a description of the car or the license number:

- Weaving across the road
- Keeping his or her face close to the windshield
- Driving off the road
- Swerving or turning suddenly
- Stopping for no reason in the middle of traffic
- Following other cars too closely
- Ignoring traffic signals
- Sudden speeding up or slowing down
- Driving without headlights when dark

To prove that alcohol impairs vision, these students try to walk a line while wearing "beer goggles," which simulate the visual effects of intoxication.

Don't feel like you're being a tattletale; you're most likely going to save lives. Never try to engage a drunk driver with your car because the impaired driver may crash into you or run you off the road. Allow the police to stop the driver you spotted. Alerting them is all you need to do.

Other Drugs

Alcohol is not the only drug that interferes with safe driving. Any drug, whether it's illegal, prescription, or over-the-counter, can slow your reaction time, cause confusion, alter your perception of objects around you, and make you drowsy or hyperactive. Drugs can also reduce your peripheral vision. These side effects will affect your driving skills and make driving very dangerous.

Some over-the-counter medicines can affect your ability to function normally. Adding just a little bit of alcohol to medication can make bad side effects worse, increasing drowsiness, wooziness, and loss of perception. Following are some descriptions of other drugs. If you become involved with any of these drugs, you take risks with all aspects of your life—your health, your mental stability, your family, your relationships, your present, and your future. Don't drive if you're taking drugs.

Hallucinogens alter your perceptions and make you lose your ability to distinguish between what is real and what is imagined. Hallucinogens include PCP, or phencyclidine, and LSD, or acid.

Stimulants speed up the activities of the cells in the central nervous system. They boost your mood. The effect is only temporary, and you'll end up more tired and low than when you started. Caffeine and nicotine are examples of stimulants that occur naturally in plants.

Amphetamines are artificial stimulants. They speed up your heart rate and other functions. They cause restlessness, shaking, sleeplessness, nervousness, memory lapses, hallucinations, and blurred vision. Ecstasy and crystal meth are examples.

Sedatives slow down the body's functioning, so your blood pressure, heart rate, breathing, and cell function drop. An overdose can cause death.

Narcotics induce sleep or sluggishness and relieve pain. They slow down your respiratory system. If you take too much of a narcotic, your oxygen intake can become so low that you die. Codeine, heroin, morphine, and Demerol are narcotics. These drugs are addictive if abused.

Even drugs prescribed by your doctor can be dangerous when combined with driving. Instructions such as "do not operate heavy machinery" are often disregarded because a car is not assumed to be "heavy machinery," but it is. University of Iowa researchers have found that even taking simple antihistamines for allergies can impair drivers. Such medications affect your ability to steer and stay in the correct lane. Ask your doctor if the medication you've been given causes drowsiness, dizziness, loss of coordination, or other side effects.

Myths and Facts

If you drink only beer, you won't get as drunk.
Fact ➡ Alcohol is alcohol, whether it's in beer, wine, or liquor. Twelve ounces of beer, five ounces of wine, and one and one-half ounces (a shot) of hard liquor all have the same amount of alcohol and are equally intoxicating. According to Mothers Against Drunk Driving (MADD), 80 percent of alcohol-related fatalities are caused by beer consumption, so you're not any safer behind the wheel by drinking beer instead of other alcoholic beverages.

You won't get drunk on a full stomach, and eating makes it easier to sober up. Fact ➡ Any food that's in your stomach will only delay the time it takes alcohol to get into the bloodstream. It won't stop the alcohol from getting there. Eventually, and with large amounts of alcohol, you will feel its full effects. You also can't sober a person up; the only thing that works is time. Cold showers, hot coffee,

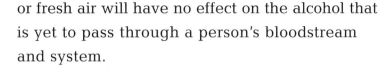

or fresh air will have no effect on the alcohol that is yet to pass through a person's bloodstream and system.

I'm a skilled driver, so I can drive home a little buzzed.

Fact ➡ According to the American Automobile Association (AAA), it takes five years of driving to become as good as the average driver. So even if you or your friends feel skilled, you've got a long way to go. In those five years, young drivers learn to judge tricky situations and acquire the skills necessary to deal with them.

In 2004, 57 percent of fatal car crashes involved only one vehicle, according to the National Highway Traffic Safety Administration (NHTSA). So while you may not hit someone else's car, odds are still high that you might end up killing yourself or your passengers. Even hitting a tree, parked car, pole, or fire hydrant can be deadly.

A drink or two actually calms me down and makes me concentrate better behind the wheel.

Fact ➡ This is a physical impossibility; your skills can only deteriorate (get worse) under the influence of alcohol. Alcohol—even a small amount—dulls your senses and reflexes, impairs your vision, and makes you more easily distracted.

WHY DO TEENS DRINK AND DRIVE?

Simplistic messages like "Just Say No" don't mean much to a teen who drinks because he or she likes the sensation or are using alcohol to escape from problems. These are complicated issues, and they need more in-depth solutions. Check out the following reasons why teens drink, according to the PBS program *Just One Night*. You'll notice that the percentages overlap, which means teens say there is more than one reason for drinking:

79 percent drink because "being drunk/high feels good."

67 percent drink because it helps to forget problems.

66 percent drink because others do it or are telling them to do it.

47 percent drink because there is nothing else to do.

Talk to an elder you trust—a parent, a teacher, an older sibling—if you think that you're developing an alcohol problem. They're not there to judge but to help.

If you are drinking, talk with a parent or guardian, a trusted teacher, the school counselor or nurse, a doctor, or even a religious leader about it. Alcohol isn't the best solution for any reason because it will prevent you from growing and developing normally. Studies show that your brain undergoes great changes and growth until somewhere around age twenty-five. In fact, some of the most dramatic brain growth, during which the brain gets bigger and thought processes get more complex and efficient, occurs during adolescence. This is why it's better to postpone the search for a good "buzz"—for whatever reasons—until you're of legal age.

It is not clear whether or to what extent the brain is able to recover from damage done by teenage drinking. However, studies clearly show that when the onset of alcohol abuse occurs later in life, cognitive functions of the brain develop more fully.

I Thought I Was Fine

Jacob Bennett, a high school senior from Madison, Wisconsin, found out the hard way that drinking and driving is the wrong thing to do. In 2006, Bennett told NBC news, "That's the last thing I remember. I don't even remember going to that party." He was with his friend Shawn Williams, and they were drinking. In their rural community, he said,"that's all there is to do." When they left the party, Shawn was at the wheel, and Jacob was in the back of the truck.

Shawn, driving drunk, veered off the road and hit a tree. The truck burst into flames. Witnesses saw Jacob running down the field, on fire. Both of his ankles were broken, yet he was unaware. While recovering in the hospital, he was told that Shawn died at the crash scene. Jacob will never talk to his bud again because he and Shawn made the fatal decision to drive drunk. Jacob has now decided to become a counselor to help prevent teens from making bad choices.

If you recognize any of the following situations when deciding whether to drive after you have been drinking, stop and think. Hand the keys to someone sober, or call for an adult to come get you and your friends. If you've had a drop of alcohol, do not drive.

Overconfident Drunk

Alcohol makes us unable to recognize what's really happening with our bodies. You might think, "I feel fine, I can handle it." This is a physical impossibility; your skills can only get worse under the influence of alcohol. You'll confuse dangerous risks with fun and excitement, and you might end up dead.

Rationalizing at the Wheel

You might tell yourself that home is only five minutes away, or no one is out on the road right now, or you've done this a hundred times before and never had a problem. Just remember Jacob and Shawn's true story—they hit a tree. On any trip, there are hundreds of things that can occur, and you don't have the driving skills necessary to react quickly and properly if you've been drinking.

Scared of Getting Caught

You've been drinking and now it's time to go, but you're so drunk. Your parents don't know that you drink. You fear that they'll be furious. This is no reason to get behind the wheel. Call a taxi, find a sober driver to take you home, or call your parents

This driving simulator teaches students just how difficult it is to control a large vehicle while driving drunk, which is something to think about before getting behind the wheel.

to come and get you. Believe this: Your parents would rather be disappointed but still have you alive than be the reason why you chose to drink and drive.

Scared of Being Lame

If you don't have a license, you might ask a friend to drive you to a party, but what can you do if your friend is drunk when it's time to go home? You know that it's wrong to get in the car with a driver who has been drinking, but telling him or her not to drive could make you feel like a nag. This situation is not easy to deal with. However, keep in mind that feeling like a nag is only a temporary situation, and temporarily feeling lame is better than being dead or maimed for life.

Making the right decision could mean the difference between life and death. If your drunk friend insists on driving, do all you can to convince him or her that it's not the smart thing to do. If possible, take away the car keys. Try not to be angry or judgmental, but gently insist that you and your friend get in a taxi or take a bus. If that's impossible, find a sober driver who can bring you both home. The next morning, your friend will realize that you were a real friend

Though peer pressure to drink and drive may be strong, your friends will ultimately respect you more if you stand your ground and choose to be the responsible one.

and made the right call. In the end, the truly lame thing to do is get behind the wheel after drinking.

Some safe ride programs for students have you and your parents sign an agreement that says you will never get in a car with a driver who has been drinking. These "contracts" can make it easier for you to deal with a potentially dangerous driver. Understandably, a friend might take it personally if you say, "You're drunk. I'm not riding with you." However, most people will understand your position if you say, "I promised my mother/ father/parents that I'd never ride in a car if the driver has had a drop of alcohol." By doing this, you are not nagging or attacking your friend personally but keeping a promise to your parents.

Poor Planning

A lot of people go to a party knowing that they are going to drink or take drugs, but they don't bother to arrange for a place to stay or a sober friend to take them home. If they try to drive themselves home, this is a disaster in the making. Some events, such as prom, pose a greater risk for spontaneous decisions with bad consequences. According to Mothers Against Drunk Driving (MADD), in 2005, 74 percent of teens polled said they were pressured to drink on prom night. About 57 percent were pressured to drive recklessly. If you plan to party, plan also to sleep over, call a taxi, take the bus, or get a ride home from a designated driver.

What About Your Friends?

Depending on your crowd, your friends may not drink, may drink once in a while, or may drink often and push drinking as a requirement to stay in the cool crowd. While you may gain "friends," you'll experience trouble with your family and loved ones, your grades, your health, and even with the law. You will also be putting yourself into life-threatening situations, such as overdoses and car accidents. Are the people who are encouraging you to make this trade-off really your friends? Would a friend really ask you to place your relationships, health, and life in jeopardy?

Ten Great Questions to Ask Your Guidance Counselor

1 Is there a safe ride program at our school?

2 If I get stopped on the highway after consuming a little bit of alcohol, what should I do (or not do)?

3 I can't tell my parents about this party I am going to. What other adult can I call if there is a problem?

4 My friend drives drunk. Should I tell his or her parents?

5 My friend's parent gives us liquor. Who should I tell?

6 I think my friend's older sibling drinks before driving us places. What's the best way to confront him or her about this?

7 I drink sometimes. What else is there to do to have fun?

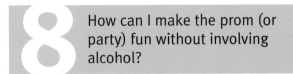

How can I make the prom (or party) fun without involving alcohol?

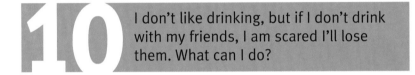

My parents drink and drive, so how can I make sure they will honor our Contract for Life?

I don't like drinking, but if I don't drink with my friends, I am scared I'll lose them. What can I do?

WHAT ARE
THE LAWS?

A simple night of drinking suddenly becomes a much bigger problem when the law is involved. The legal minimum drinking age across the United States is twenty-one. Each state has its own penalties for breaking this law. The law is "bent" only for the purposes of established religious customs. Common penalties for the underage drinker for a first-time offense include:

Probation: you regularly check in with an officer, who monitors your sobriety for a period of months or years.

Appearing in juvenile court.

Suspended driving privileges for 30 to 180 days.

Fines, ranging between $500 and $2,000.

Community service.

Mandatory program attendance: alcohol education, drivers education, drug rehabilitation.

If you've been found guilty of this offense for a second or third time, you may face jail time. Parents or guardians who make alcohol available to a minor could be fined thousands of dollars and spend up to a year in jail.

If you're not drinking but have liquor in your possession, you're still subject to be charged and fined. If you're not drinking but go to a party where there is liquor, you're still not legally out of the woods. The police can charge you—and the party's hosts.

Taking It to the Streets: A Bad Idea

The penalties for drunk driving are severe. The charge is commonly called driving under the influence, or DUI. It may also be called driving while intoxicated (DWI), operating under the influence (OUI), or operating a motor vehicle intoxicated (OMVI). The charge may mean that you're driving in an impaired manner due to alcohol or drugs, or that you're driving with alcohol or drugs in your system, no matter how you're driving—safely or otherwise.

Fines, Penalties, and Loss

You'll probably be assessed a fine if you're caught drinking and driving. Fines differ in each state. In Indiana and Washington, for instance, you have to pay a fine of up to $5,000. Other penalties for underage drunk driving include the following and vary per state as to severity and duration:

- Seizure of your license
- Seizure of your car
- Mandatory drug and alcohol rehabilitation
- Mandatory drivers' classes
- Probation
- Jail

A lawyer may have to represent you in court. If you're found guilty, the fines will be hefty. In addition, not having a license or car can affect your employment and school life. A charge of driving under the influence (DUI) is a criminal offense that goes on your record. Few employers feel comfortable hiring someone who has been convicted of impaired driving. You just won't come across as trustworthy.

With a DUI, your parents' insurance carrier will most likely drop your policy. It will be extremely difficult to find another company that will insure you unless you pay very high premiums. Without insurance, you can't drive, and with a DUI, you're now considered a risk not worth taking.

Crime and Jail Time

One driving under the influence (DUI) charge may keep you out of the driver's seat for years. If you hurt or kill someone while driving drunk, you can be charged with a felony. A felony is a serious crime, like rape or murder. Jail time starts with a minimum of one year depending on the state and the nature of your crime. The family of the person or people you hurt may also sue you or your family.

With drinking and driving such a deadly problem, the penalties are severe, ranging from serious fines and suspension of license to jail time.

You should know that more people are being arrested and sentenced to jail time for DUI than ever before. According to the National Center for Injury Prevention and Control, in 2004, 1.4 million drivers were arrested for driving while impaired. This is 1 out of every 135 drivers. Jail time for this offense varies per state. For example, in Washington, there's a minimum of twenty-four consecutive hours in jail, and a maximum period of one year. In Delaware, the minimum is sixty days and the maximum is six months.

Your youth won't get you off the hook either. According to the Substance Abuse and Mental Health Services

Administration (SAMHSA), 169,000 teens aged sixteen to twenty reported that they were arrested and booked for DUI during 2002 and 2003.

In the Eyes of the Law

If you drive under the influence of alcohol or drugs, you are a criminal. That may not seem fair, but think about it. You are operating a very heavy machine that is moving at high speeds. Operating a vehicle when drunk turns the already risky activity of driving into criminally reckless behavior. The DWI and DUI laws are in place to protect innocent people from getting hurt or killed by a driver who's not in control because of reckless decisions.

If you are pulled over because a police officer suspects you of DUI, you will be tested for the presence of alcohol in your system. Your blood alcohol concentration (BAC) will be tested with a Breathalyzer or similar breath-testing instrument. You may also have to take a field sobriety test, for which you must walk a straight line or perform other tasks that reveal if your coordination is impaired. If you refuse to cooperate, your license can be suspended immediately.

If the police suspect that you're on other drugs, you may be taken to a trained drug recognition tester, who will put you through tests to see if you're clean. You'll be tested for such things as the reaction of your pupils to light, the speed of your pulse, quivering eyelids, bloodshot eyes, muscle rigidity, and needle scars.

Even taking one drink can put you over the legal limit. With zero tolerance laws, you may be faced with prosecution for driving when you thought you were sober.

Zero Tolerance Laws

According to the Insurance Information Institute, every state defines a blood alcohol concentration (BAC) of .08 as drunk driving. When a person tests .08 or higher, they are considered to be illegally operating a vehicle and are subject to punishment. In order to reach .08, a 170-pound male would have to consume about four drinks in one hour on an empty stomach. A 137-pound female would have to consume three drinks in an hour.

A Breathalyzer is a machine that measures how much you've had to drink. You may be able to fool your parents, but you can't trick the machine.

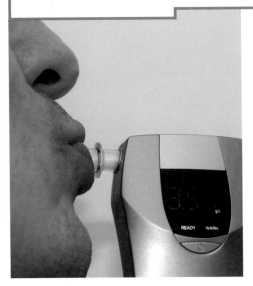

Lawmakers have taken measures with your peer group in mind. All states have enacted the zero tolerance law. Anyone under twenty-one who is caught driving after drinking even one sip of alcohol is subject to fines, arrest, jail time, and other penalties. It doesn't matter if your BAC is .01 or .03—you're busted! In some states, you're arrested immediately at the time of being stopped by police.

When you're pulled over on suspicion of drunk driving, you'll be asked to breathe into a Breathalyzer or other similar breath-testing device. Taking breath mints—contrary to popular belief—will not "fool" the devices. Sucking on a penny will not fool the device either. While it may seem foolproof, there are cases where devices such as the Breathalyzer are wrong. On rare occasions, a person's BAC may read .08 percent or even higher when he or she was not drinking at all. This is called a false-positive result. You may also be intoxicated, but the test will show a BAC of 0.0 percent. This is a false-negative result.

There are different explanations for a false-positive reading, including faulty testing devices. Some devices cannot detect the difference between ethyl alcohol and similar compounds found in mouthwash or some oral medications. People who use asthma inhalers sometimes test positive even if they haven't consumed any alcohol. If you haven't been drinking but are tested and show a high BAC, insist on being tested again in fifteen minutes. Anyone who shows a high BAC will be taken back to the station. There, you'll be given another, more advanced breath test to rule out false-positives. You may also give a sample of your blood and urine for further testing. If you haven't consumed any alcohol, these other tests should prove your innocence.

HOW DO I PREVENT THE WORST FROM HAPPENING?

If you use alcohol or drugs and then get behind the wheel, the consequences can be fatal. All it takes is a split second. One of the best things you can do to show that you value your life and the lives of people in your community is to vow never to get behind the wheel of a car when you are impaired. In addition, do your best to prevent your friends or family members from doing so. By trying to ensure that your immediate circle of friends and family always drives safely, you will already cut down the chances that drunk driving will devastate your group.

If you do end up getting dragged to a party where you know that alcohol will be served, make sure that you have a designated driver. A designated driver is someone who goes to the party but will not consume any liquor or drugs. His or her job is to round up your buds and deposit you all safely at home at the end of the evening. Treat your designated driver like a prince or princess by serving him or her nonalcoholic cocktails and munchies. Because fair is fair, you can offer to be the designated driver on the next occasion.

Safe Driving: Awareness Is Key

It doesn't hurt to be the smartest or most mature teen in your group. Understanding the risks and dangers of alcohol use—and abuse—will help save lives. Let's face it: alcohol is always going to be around, and dealing with it is a part of growing up. If you're the voice of reason when your friends want to party, that's okay. It will allow your friends to have many more happy memories.

Don't be afraid to tell your friend not to get behind the wheel. Don't be afraid to call someone when you and your friends need a ride. Don't be afraid to show that you have knowledge and power to saves lives.

Keep in mind these statistics from the National Highway Traffic Safety Administration (NHTSA):

When you're handed keys to a car, you're being given a great responsibility, which includes being mature enough to say no to drinking and driving.

➡️ **Summer:** More car-crash teen fatalities happen during the summer than any other season.

➡️ **Weekends:** More alcohol-related crashes occur on Saturdays and Sundays than during weekdays.

➡️ **Late nights:** About 76 percent of fatal car crashes between midnight and 3 AM involve alcohol. Saturday and Sunday from midnight to 3 AM are the deadliest hours.

➡️ **Speed:** More than half of all fatal crashes occur on roads where the speed limit is 55 mph or higher because people tend to drive much faster.

➡️ **Objects:** Collisions with fixed objects account for 43 percent of fatal crashes.

In addition to knowing the facts about drinking and driving, there are many ways you can get together with others to improve the safety of everyone on the road. Here are a few examples:

Project Graduation

Project Graduation is a national alcohol-safety program designed to keep kids safe, healthy, and alive during prom and graduation. This program:

➡️ Has teens sign pledges not to drink or do drugs and drive

➡️ Sets up a safe ride system

➡️ Promotes "Buckle-Up Day"

If your school does not have a Project Graduation in place, contact your state's Department of Education. Representatives

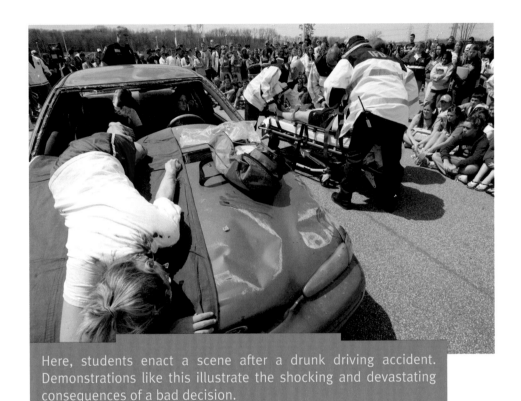

Here, students enact a scene after a drunk driving accident. Demonstrations like this illustrate the shocking and devastating consequences of a bad decision.

will guide you on how to establish Project Graduation at your school.

Students Against Destructive Decisions

Students Against Destructive Decisions (SADD) is an organization for high school students who want to do something about the deadly combination of drinking and driving. SADD is made up of locally run chapters. In 1981, Robert Anastas, director of health education in the Wayland public schools in Massachusetts organized the program in his schools. The idea spread quickly. You can start a chapter at your school if you don't already have one.

SADD has an agreement called the Contract for Life. You and your parents or guardian sign a contract in which you both agree to be responsible for your safety. You agree that you will always ride with a sober driver and buckle your seat belt. In dangerous situations, you also agree to contact your parents or guardian to pick you up. They agree to pick you up at any time, day or night, no questions asked. This contract helps to build trust between you and the people who love you and care about your safety.

Safe Rides for Teens

Many schools have a safe ride program. It is usually run by students, parents, teachers, and other volunteers. If you or your ride home is drunk, you can call and a volunteer on call will give you a lift home. If you don't have a safe ride program at your school, talk to a teacher or guidance counselor to get one started.

Organize an Assembly

Sometimes the best way to reach people is through a personal story. Organize an assembly with speakers who have suffered because of underage drunk driving. Local police and safety commissions can do a car-crash demonstration. Distribute materials on alcohol and its addictive nature, and how it affects

To find out more about preventing drinking and driving, turn to organizations like SADD, Students Against Destructive Decisions, which offer literature on the subject.

our decision making. There are also movies, such as the California Highway Patrol's *Red Asphalt,* that show the very graphic reality of crashes.

Peer Counseling

Peer counseling is a way for students to help each other. It uses students as role models, helpers, and leaders. Many teens feel more comfortable talking about alcohol addiction with peers. Knowing that someone cares means a lot when dealing with life's problems.

alcoholic Of or containing alcohol; also, a person suffering from alcoholism.

alcoholism Chronic disease characterized by physical and psychological dependence on alcohol.

amphetamine Artificial stimulant.

blood alcohol concentration (BAC) Percentage amount of alcohol in a person's bloodstream.

Breathalyzer This is the trade name of a device used to test blood alcohol concentration (BAC) of a suspected drunk driver.

designated driver Person chosen to drive intoxicated people home based on the fact that he or she will not be drinking alcohol.

DUI Driving under the influence of drugs or alcohol.

DWI Driving while intoxicated.

ethanol (ethyl alcohol) Psychoactive substance found in liquor.

felony Serious crime.

hallucinogen Drug or chemical that causes hallucinations or distorted experiences.

intoxicated Drunk or high on drugs, resulting in reduced mental and physical control.

narcotic Drug such as morphine or heroin that dulls one's feelings and lessens pain.

OMVI Operating a motor vehicle intoxicated.

OUI Operating under the influence.

sedative Drug that calms or induces sleep.

stimulant Drug that excites or quickens the body's functioning.

Alateen

1600 Corporate Landing Parkway

Virginia Beach, VA 23454-5617

(888) 4AL-ANON [425-2666]

Web site: http://www.al-anon.alateen.org

This organization helps teens who are recovering alcoholics or have family members who are alcoholics.

Alcoholics Anonymous (AA)

Grand Central Station

P.O. Box 459

New York, NY 10163

(212) 870-3400

Web site: http://www.alcoholics-anonymous.org

This organization is made up of recovering alcoholics who strive to support one another and provide information for family members.

American Automobile Association Foundation for
  Traffic Safety

607 14th Street NW, Suite 201

Washington, DC 20005

(800) 305-SAFE [305-7233]

Web site: http://www.aaafoundation.org

This foundation's mission is to identify traffic safety problems and provide information and educational materials.

American Driver and Traffic Safety Education Association
Indiana University of Pennsylvania
R & P Building
Indiana, PA 15705
(800) 896-7703
Web site: http://www.adtsea.iup.edu/adtsea
This association creates and publishes policies for safe driving.

Center for Substance Abuse Prevention
(800) 662-HELP [662-4357]
Web site: http://www.samhsa.gov
This is part of the U.S. Substance Abuse and Mental Health Services Administration. This resource helps communities improve the quality of life through outreach.

Mothers Against Drunk Driving (MADD)
511 E. John Carpenter Freeway, Suite 700
Irving, TX 75062
(800) GET-MADD [438-6233]
(877) MADD-HELP [623-3435]
Web site: http://www.madd.org
This organization's mission is to stop drunk driving and support victims of drunk driving.

National Center on Addiction and Substance Abuse at
    Columbia University (CASA)

633 Third Avenue, 19th Floor

New York, NY 10017-6706

Web site: http://www.casacolumbia.org

(21) 841-5200

This organization provides information about substance abuse and its effects and encourages individuals to combat substance abuse in their communities.

National Highway Traffic Safety Administration (NHTSA)

400 7th Street SW

Washington, DC 20590

(888) 327-4236

Web site: http://www.nhtsa.dot.gov

This organization works to save lives, prevent injuries, and reduce crashes.

National Safety Council

1121 Spring Lake Drive

Itasca, IL 60143–3201

(630) 285-1121

Web site: http://www.nsc.org

This organization works to educate and influence people to prevent accidental injury and death.

Students Against Destructive Decisions (SADD)

255 Main Street

Marlborough, MA 01752

(877) SADD-INC (723-3462)

Web site: http://www.sadd.org

This organization will help you start your own chapter and also offers information on drunk driving on its Web site.

Web Sites

Due to the changing nature of Internet links, Rosen Publishing has developed an online list of Web sites related to the subject of this book. This site is updated regularly. Please use this link to access the list:

http://www.rosenlinks.com/faq/drdr

For Further Reading

Aaseng, Nathan. *Teens and Drunk Driving*. San Diego, CA: Lucent Books, 2000.

Cornell, Andrew. *Teenager or Adult: Do We Deserve to Drink Alcohol?* Lincoln, NE: iUniverse, Incorporated, 2005.

Gerdes, Louise I., ed. *Drunk Driving*. Farmington Hills, MI: Thomson Gale Group, 2004.

Miller, Andrew. *Alcohol and Your Liver: The Incredibly Disgusting Story*. New York, NY: The Rosen Publishing Group, Inc., 2000.

Strasser, Todd. *The Accident*. Lincoln, NE: Backinprint.com, 2006.

Tullson, Diane. *Blue Highway*. Markham, ON, Canada: Fitzhenry & Whiteside Limited, 2004.

Winters, Adam. *Everything You Need to Know About Being a Teen Driver*. New York, NY: The Rosen Publishing Group, Inc., 2000.

About the Author

Holly Cefrey is an award-winning children's book author who has written numerous books for Rosen Publishing on a variety of subjects, including health and wellness.

Photo Credits

Cover © www.istockphoto.com/Daniel Bendjy; p. 6 © Peter Hvizdak/The Image Works; pp. 8, 25, 51 © AP Images; p. 9 © www.istockphoto.com/Michael Blackburn; p. 11 © Larry Kolvoord/The Image Works; p. 13 © www.istockphoto.com/Dennis Oblander; p. 15 © Marka/Custom Medical Stock Photo; p. 18 © www.istockphoto.com/Isabel Massé; p. 20 © Marcus Mok/Asia Images/Getty Images; p. 23 © Mike Siluk/The Image Works; p. 31 © Nancy Richmond/The Image Works; pp. 34–35 © Dan Rosenstrauch/Contra Costa Times/Zuma Press; p. 36 © Bob Daemmrich/The Image Works; p. 43 © www.istockphoto.com/Wayne Howard; p. 45 © Joe Raedle/Getty Images; p. 46 © www.istockphoto.com/Tomasz Resiak; p. 49 © www.istockphoto.com/Curt Pickens; p. 53 © Ron Gould/Custom Medical Stock Photo.

Designer: Evelyn Horovicz; Photo Researcher: Amy Feinberg